THE GEORGIA POETRY PRIZE

The University of Georgia Press established
the Georgia Poetry Prize in 2016 in partnership
with the Georgia Institute of Technology,
Georgia State University, and the University of
Georgia. The prize is supported by the Bruce
and Georgia McEver Fund for the Arts and
Environment.

SUN & URN

Previous Books By Christopher Salerno

Whirligig, 2006
Minimum Heroic, 2010
ATM, 2014

SUN & URN

Christopher Salerno

*For Kit,
with Gratitude
2018*

The University of Georgia Press   *Athens*

Published by the University of Georgia Press

Athens, Georgia 30602

www.ugapress.org

© 2017 by Christopher Salerno

All rights reserved

Designed by Erin Kirk New

Set in Bell

Printed and bound by Sheridan Books, Inc.

The paper in this book meets the guidelines for
permanence and durability of the Committee on
Production Guidelines for Book Longevity of the
Council on Library Resources.

Most University of Georgia Press titles are
available from popular e-book vendors.

Printed in the United States of America

21   20   19   18   17   P   5   4   3   2   1

Library of Congress Cataloging-in-Publication Data

Names: Salerno, Christopher, 1975– author.

Title: Sun & urn / Christopher Salerno.

Other titles: Sun and urn

Description: First edition. | Athens, GA : University of Georgia
    Press, [2017] | Series: The Georgia Poetry Prize | Description
    based on print version record and CIP data provided by publisher;
    resource not viewed.

Identifiers: LCCN 2016022647 (print) | LCCN 2016016098 (ebook) |
    ISBN 9780820350486 (Ebook) | ISBN 9780820350493 (softcover :
    acid-free paper)

Classification: LCC PS3619.A435 (print) | LCC PS3619.A435 A6 2017
    (ebook) | DDC 811/.6—dc23

LC record available at https://lccn.loc.gov/2016022647

From a real body, which was there, proceed radiations which ultimately touch me, who am here; the duration of the transmission is insignificant; the photograph of the missing being will touch me like the delayed rays of a star.

~from *Camera Lucida,* by Roland Barthes

CONTENTS

THREE

ACKNOWLEDGMENTS

Thanks and acknowledgments to the journals in which some
of these poems first appeared: *Academy of American Poets Poem-
a-Day Series, Guernica, Sixth Finch, Boston Review, The Journal,
Pen America Series, Barn Owl Review, Verse Daily, Laurel Review,
Thrush, Handsome, Green Mountains Review, Prairie Schooner,* and
Gulf Coast. Some of these poems appeared in a chapbook titled,
Aorta, published in 2014 by Poor Claudia, the chapbook imprint of
Octopus Books.

Special thanks to the New Jersey State Council on the Arts for
its generous arts grant and fellowship, which helped to support
the writing of these poems. Thanks also to William Paterson
University's 2013 Humanities and Social Sciences Grant.

I am forever grateful to Thomas Lux, Kelsea Habecker, Timothy
Liu, Wyn Cooper, Nicholas Van Eck and Poor Claudia, the WPU
English Department, *Map Literary,* and the great folks at UGA
Press, all of whom helped or supported me in some way during the
making of this book.

ONE

DEDICATION

In a storefront dojo a black belt yells
at a bunch of orange belts,
something staccato about a punch
not being a punch
if it fails to inflect your luminous destiny,
your three good reasons
to punch not related to rage.
If you should only love the sound
of your fist in the air
like whipping out a small bouquet
of pink buds,
the sensei says you must also be struck
sometimes by the quiet
of nothing moving or rising up.
In the annals of that silence
make your wolf call.
In the annals of that silence always a wolf
circles just because
there is no true surface, there is no solid ground,
so better never sleep
and always a hellhound be.

IS IT BETTER WHERE YOU ARE?

The bakery's graffiti
spells either *hope* or *nope*.
But hope and results are different,
said Fanny Brawne to her Keats
voiding his unreasonable lung.
Getting off the medicine
completely means light again
blinking to light. Device returned
to its factory settings—
the complete black of before
the meteor shower
above the bakery. If you lose the smell
of leather, lemon, or rose,
studies show you will fail at being,
like Keats. I keep watching
the same meteor
shower videos on YouTube
where awe is always a question of scale.
The bakery, now, beginning to close,
my arrhythmic heart
aches for the kind of dramatic arc
one can't shop for.
To lease what's real for a while—
is that the good kind
of consumption? I wonder
over the weight of meaning,
the difference between

hull and seed. The sugary donut
and its graceful hole.
The greasy bags everyone leaves
in the alley leading to my door.
These scraps I work at like a crow.

BRAY

It's summer here so soda pop and blue
jeans in the trees. I am peeling
my sunburn on a bus bound for Saratoga
Springs where I will lob my father's
ashes on the line where the racehorses
finish one at a time, and as they do,
the mist of a million particles
of ash in the air, all likeness will disappear
between us. I had built a boundary
out of skin where I sat quietly
until blood was the only moving
thing on a map of where we are.
On the dirt track, horses fill
their lungs in the sun and urge on.
When a losing horse dips
its head to greet me, his black whiskers
tickle the flesh of my neck. Why
do all hearted creatures stink?
I am asked by my brother's
youngest child, *Is horse your favorite*
or least favorite mammal? I say
don't beg the Lord if the sky is
a gray roof beneath which
you have waited all day to see
gallop something graceful, swift.

IRRESPONSIBILITY

It's too easy
to be the ancient Chinese pupil
disobeying his master,
to hide, tucked inside a single bluebell
on a meadow obscured
by hoof prints. Right now
I have done something so wrong
to the oxcart
the ox refuses to move.
Cracked, too, the moon and the phone.
Spring, and the sound
of thunder without
lightning. I only heard it once,
like childhood. A river gone
red from what was
in the sod. No clear water
to wash one's hat strings. No hollow
bamboo noise or subtitles
or starlings to memorize.
Just cherries burning the meadow
grass like the bombs
we grew up with. I gather
them before dark,
wanting only to work
like a flower, to push
just barely
my variety of honey.

THE TALKING FORCE FIELD

It's only me blasting
a podcast of night
as I sip my Moscow
mule, stare out at the black
sea of ferns where I will set
fire to my dead father's
toupee in the overgrown
yard beside the live oak
I like to climb with my niece
and her newborn dolls,
bald with pink brains,
where my nephew and I
swing tinfoil machetes
and pretend to hack
each other's limbs.
Nothing is real: Wind is
not wind. Air is not air.
These are not my initials
shaved into the side
of this wolf. This earth
is not a MILF. But climb
the man and you
will find Romanticism—
climb higher and you
will reach a word cloud
that reads: *I am very sick*
but don't yet know it.

BLACK HOLES

No stars now
because tree. Maple
leafing out against
the house. It's a shame
to mourn alone. I am
a mammal. There are eight
or more openings in
my body. I had previously
forgotten the three
that don't make any noise,
how our night holes
become day holes. Let me see
if I can understand you
as an opening, my ear
cocked to the air. Why
are we still whispering?
People say to age into
the epoch, that trying
to change a fraction of
the past is hard, like math.
I go to the window
where the laws of nature
are sometimes writ
on leaves like love letters
floating up, star-deep
into all the black holes.

REAL OR IN EFFIGY

Look at
our father. Daily baby
aspirin in him. Arteries
with tiny apertures. Dead
in his bed. They wake
me. Do I want to see
him one last time? Sixty-one
years with a shame of being
seen without his lifts and wig.
My brother discovered
the body at dawn. TV bolted
above. Case of Bud
Light making metaphors
of thirst. The silver way one's final
lumens glow. Over, now,
the burden of willing
the self awake every day.
He left behind marijuana,
a small gray suit
of smoke for me. Black rubber
blood pressure. Metal chairs on top
of his beach house where
one could spot a migrating whale
willing to breach. Left behind
a sigh of relief. His sick
dog to bark. Some lights

on upstairs when
he died, a slumped-
over body waving
to itself.

PRESSED FOR DETAILS

There are ways to say *die*
without a findable body. My neighbor
hauls a female mannequin
to the open dumpster. Somebody's dug
a hole in her crotch, rimmed
in black magic marker. I feel a team
of butterflies rise up. Standing
on a pile of breakaway glass, I blow
into my cupped hands for warmth
the way one would on a dark playground,
its poplars tall and parallel like
the person one is meant to become:
old enough to offer one's physical self
as proof of life. To the detective I reply,
This is where I lose the thread.
I thought dying was like a privacy. After
they carried my father's body
away, I sat forever in his open garage:
golf bags, bags of concrete dust.
Spiders living in his bicycle frame
setting sail in their webs.

SUN & URN

What are the patterns that distinguish us from ghosts?
I tan.
You rock
back and forth.
Our lease is nearly up.

We touch the grass, play the toy piano rooted in the mud,
our heads back as if swallowing bells.

A cloud arrives, opens and then closes.

I am ready to *not* see the light.

*

Do you think death's effect is
of entering or being entered? Like waking but
at the wrong hour?

When the world was flat, that didn't happen.

People slept all the time. They thought the world was wider.
　Thought that words

set to music would take refuge in music. Not be like bottle rockets
or fast growing trees.

This is a season too.

*

With some, near the end, there is a farewell
act of awareness—a smile, a robin's egg

returned gently to its nest
in the satellite dish.

This explains the feather in my grandfather's death cap!

I once asked him
about the size of the world.
Are you wanting to possess it? he asked.

No, but I anthropomorphize
animals in landscapes. See in the trees expectant
parent squirrels returning
to their nests at night,
finally less visible.

*

My brother over
the phone asks me if
I'm sitting down. I stand. Remember how he
once in a park broke

another boy's arm by snapping an elbow up.
That boy sat down.

Now I am standing. Language begins.
I sit back down. I am a flag
with two heights.

Do you think it (death) is supposed to come as a surprise?
Like the moon claiming you?

*

I can hear
men hammering on a nearby roof
today. Some tree fruit sways overhead

like a traffic light. Lord,
     stop me.
What I started to say. About urging
the ill to come forward,
try to die.

THE GRADUAL AGING OF EVERYONE INVOLVED

I have heard about a fountain of youth, and I will try
to touch for a second
the relay from him who carried me on his back
and taught me every obscenity.
Even the real gods
seemed to know my name
from the moment I woke the swans with a stone.

But the life of a swan is a stint on a pond.
Some stasis. Lots of waiting.
For two hours I looked
across at a fountain flanked by two curves of ice
like a lifespan in parentheses.

You can wait your
whole life, skinny limbs reaching
over a body of water, and misunderstand
the ways beauty persuades you.

Prefer instead the dreams
of strangers. The empty pond dappled by
the stammering of day.
Or how sometimes people leave
and leave a small
boat drifting.

HALLOWEEN

You were a white cocoon shot through with gravel.
I was a knocked-down nest.
We are unassailable only insofar as we produce
in the end something beautiful.
Luna, outside are monsters in parked cars.
Not you. Not when I have just set my preferences
for the twenty-first century.
Ghost messages from the end of our tenure
tell me of more boredom. A generally
birdless evening. Bakery paper spirals
in high wind. Neighbors I don't know
arrive home from work. Thousands
of other lives, pixels in the burning design
imprinted at birth on the brain
with our innate love of death.
Here's an idea someone had in a cemetery,
its headstones tall and ordered:
to take careful steps, the way ghosts do
when they are starting to assemble,
or when crossing from hell,
beyond the beautiful boundary.

COHABITING

That circular shape of the nest is made

 by the body of the bird turning around,

pressing against the walls of the nest.

 Formation always comes before form,

like our fingernails, an endless revision,

 or eventual sex, a mark on the bed,

a forehead smudge on the windowpane.

 Outward we press, our shapes suggesting

no wonder: a song for each agony

 recorded on the body, whorled or worse.

IN VITRO

More snow fell than was able

to be plowed. We turned

our faces to the clouds, waited

in waiting rooms to fill

out the forms, kissing each

one like the scalp of a child

with hair as unreal

as a doll built by hand

in the hold of a beautiful ship.

I sit in the room full of porn,

exhale my own name,

the one of that saint who

carried the Christ child

over a swollen river.

FURNACE

The plumber's apprentice says to bleed
the furnace every few weeks.
I don't know
what "bleeding" means.
My neighbor's house
is wrapped in Tyvek. Work trucks surround
a hole in the ground. I steal
scrap copper from the job site. A little
copper bird for her,
a little copper bird for me.
We live
with the absence of strong male metaphor,
the empty bed
of a white pickup truck.
All winter
it was so wintery
I was lost
in the driveway. My dad that December
would be dead very soon.
A woodpecker hammered at the boxwood.
The woodpecker's song
was about us
nailing something in.

THE EVENING REPORT

I wake up remembering that words are tries.
You want me to check your head for ticks.
There are multiple crickets in the laundry room.
I have a new plan to rid the moisture from my watch.
We are matter-of-factly still not pregnant.
You are heading to jury duty in downtown Newark.
The starlings do their thing like a scarf in the wind.
The neighbor's having trouble with his Chevy
Silverado. I am falling in love with the material world.
I tried to crush a tick with two Bayer aspirins.
I found a pair of crutches during last night's storm.
Today the tree is my exit and the sky is my porn.
I titled your drawing, "Bug with Orange Brains."
You took your coat off and put it back on.
The sun was setting in the legs of your dress.
Everyone was right about returning to the breath.
The deer were undone and lying in the grass.
We wanted to be smiling and in awe of the deer.
We stayed awake all night until everything was wet.

WHAT'S UP?

The thing is
even after a rain
the nature of nature written
in the syntax of summer
contains more pheromones
than the trimmings of hair
poets will leave for birds
to weave into their nests this spring.
When Rilke said poetry is
a centaur, he meant look
at all of those torsos—
how convergence, not distance
is the more startling medium
when the color of the sky is
what in life terrifies. Turning
all red, one cloud is
gathering like a fucked-up paw.
Is there another word
for always talking about doubt—
the voice like fabric?
If it turns out to be *prayer*
I'm not here.

IN VITRO

The pinhole camera

keeping its eye

on the seagull folding

refolding one wing

to the beat of a lullaby

titled *Father Of No One*

I imagine the slosh

of a million swimmers

stitching the ocean

choosing that love

over the peninsula

packed with fat seals

lying side by side

like fertility dolls

there's no point in looking

I do what I hate

do it in a dark condo-

minium by the sea

where it skirts the cliff

I cum into a cup

white American gull

time to kiss.

IN MEDIAS RES

Forty turns mother-

hood off. Death to all

that kid-shaped contour.

I flex to make my

fake tattoo move. You

spit-take your daiquiri,

make the ants come.

TWO

PLOT

I have not wasted my life
if the moon has risen

over my Toyota. A moon
spectral in its rising

above the municipal pond
parking lot where a turtle

on its back grapples
with the pavement, or torpor,

as the high-pressure sodium
lights burn above like two TVs.

I am held together by wire,
my grandmother confides in me

as we slow dance on
a roadside full of edible flowers—

1-2-3 from where we are
to where we are not.

To say someone is missing is
to measure the unoccupied space.

To see not them but
because of them. A whole valley

from a station wagon window.
As with any plot: we read

into movement the history
of kinetics. Read into

blank pastures the chapters
of unwritten books.

THE CASUALTIES

Horror
never stops promising.
Near the picnic shelter: thighbones, a lighter, an aerosol can.
A bottle rocket smoldering in a pine straw nest.
We have either passed through the forest
or we are passing through.

I slept beneath
a black tarp until the dew rested barely on top.
But I did not root down. I lay flat
as a cassette tape resting on a stone.
I heard seed pods dropping on the tarp. Saw the eyelids of a leaf.

I'd lost my phone and ran
as fast as I could to the spot where I'd sketched
the weird skull and spine.
Like the darkness in my heart, it was no longer there.
Gone like a green-headed fly
into new air or a hole in the sky.

What is up
with everyone now saddled with dread?
The campfire dying, it's me and my two cousins covering their eyes.
Nobody dares walk back
to the truck. I pretend in their presence
to hear a stick snap.

NIGH

The alpha day and the omega day
then the shrubs all smelled disgusting
when morning came
an eighteen wheeler rode
by and cleared the yard of starlings
they had filled it so completely
our religious neighbor up and coughing
what couldn't be discussed in words
so many wineglasses to be washed
and put away on felt pads, remember
this is a place of civility
the outside yard a large lit-up room
with an unhealthy fig tree
where six ripe figs hung
until I placed them in a hatbox
and left it for the neighbor who
likes kites and Iggy Pop.

IN VITRO

Around the wreck of

the Titanic lay nine

grand pianos swaying

with the tides to the closing

notes of a Chopin

nocturne played

by the daughter I thought

I would have.

A HISTORY OF NOISE

Plainsong, I can't hear you
over the clatter of jackhammers
sketching a surface first thing,
morning, and buildermen acting like
something's about to be sawed
in the narrow stone alley between
the church convent and our bordering bed
of Double Late Tulips opening
now too wide to go on living. They'll miss
the history of noise built up
into statement: so little mercy
for those kept from sleep. We doze
back until light hits the fig trees
in four-color, the earth now out
of its lull. Disquietude, that's a word
with a dial, the high-fidelity
sound of steel throttling concrete.
Hell: day's wide load brings
another refrain: *We make less love*
than we do new ways to frame it.

THE BIG DAY

I hold a pile of shaving cream
no one else has held. The words
dissolve in water. Never mind
I'm in a tuxedo. I have no idea
what I'm doing. I drank a vial of
something black. Tea, I think.
I once smelled a tangerine blossom
from the other side of the world.
It must be bright there, all the fruit
cut into stars. Beekeepers standing
in a blizzard of bees. Somebody
weave me a veil like that! I, too,
want to try in the sun. I'm not a tree
saying certain words, but there's a ton
of light to the east that I need.
And you, there, wearing your white—
sorry I'm so fast. This fever I talk
about is entire. With it I am
tying my formal tie. Do you take
this hand and its quivering germ?
In the name of skin and hives
we stand here with our shaves.

FOUND

My one lost glove
in the lawn come spring.
Soon I will spot
from before we were born
the walkway stones
like proven theories leading
people to this home
where I cough out candles
and thicken my waist.
Like the landscape, I will learn
to heap. A sack filled
with slick, black leaves—
I will bear it with a hunch.
Scrawl *MINE TO KEEP*
in pollen along the roadside,
its dead marsupials bloodier
than blood. What I will miss
is the long crawl back
to health. We can always make up
for the silence, but for
the lack of words? People quoting
people we should have become
by now. I am reminded of May's
other immediacies: geese
migrating above, the sound
of a two-stroke
engine down the block,
or that familiar bark

of distress: some outdoor dog
whose demons are in charge.
In Detroit after the thaw
they found forty-seven
dogs, all still frozen in
the prim light of spring.

HELIUM

Every day, the afterlife.
Deceased people's
profiles staying active
forever. We wear black
beneath our shirts in case
of a wake, neoprene
capes we will use to rise.
It is easier to love
those who are gone.

*

On a day of national remembrance,
emoticons keep comfort alive.
A jet plane and a yellow sun.
Deer everywhere. We'd easily survive
a plague of butterflies,
but a plague of downed kites?
It's only September. We watch
campus construction,
workers digging something up.

*

I beg the Canadian
geese to dip down
to the water, be the ghosts

that skim the thin ice
from the university pond,
to please hold
the clouds, take this fat
glare from my eyes.

*

Some say the sky is still
a bruise, that only the perfect
angle keeps airplanes
in the air. We eat
at the little restaurant
that won't mop up.
Police on every corner today.
A fatherly world
in a lot of ways. Its radio voices.

*

"A bear has been spotted
on campus." All activity
is postponed. Nothing
but the bear full-stride
in the quad. We scrub
ourselves until we have
no smell, like clover flower.
Some poems are

remembrances. Some
do voodoo.

*

What I have memorized
is moving again. I hear it
behind what I mean. I dare you
to name another animal.
Loneliness? Luck
in absentia? This is now
a novel. We have learned
to move silently across
the quad. Learned the calculus
of furred things, of re-
incarnation and nerve. I dream
of a mother bear
who wants me dead. Always
more ghosthood. I will soon be
a silhouette. Say farewell
to Christopher.

DIVORCE POX

Falls always on a body, with the same
dumb abundance of a rose filled with snow.
It's the waywardness of our weather
now. This must be all there is
today: the pinecones and the neighbor
child. The color of my true
love's nails. Our eyes still function
with prescription. But clearness of purpose
is no guarantee of coming to
any surface. Maybe love governs.
The red diary, carved lotus
on the cover, is temporarily shelved.
But our color can change. It's also
in the sick. Knowing time is knowing
why the cardinal cannot choose
just one branch under
the pouring sky. All April long
in the tree that never was.

SEDENTARY IS TIRING TOO

The manhole
 cover bangs
  as the plow
 drives over it. Birds
rise and reset. What I have
 memorized is

moving again. The winter
 sun hitting the sub-
  station fence—a rubric
 for evening. If I leave
 my body now to watch
reality TV alone

I will have missed some-
 thing straining after
its own vanishment. How
 in the end we loom.
 Later, I try will-
ing that moment

back into being,
 but it's late I am full
  like the canoe
 packed with snow,
  a thing you only row
 with your eyes.

TWO RED ASPIRIN

You can have the opposite
of amnesia
                and what
      that is
      is grief.
      You start a day
      with the perfect wound.
If art
is true
you have no food.
No appetite. This
is difficult—

the sad heart wants
to constellate
              or marry white
all winter. The cold metal

core not the
least bit shining.

Until a daffodil
      blooms just below
           the scalp—
      we put our grief, its infinity
      down. Finally

hungry, we park
        behind the diner
                like rats.

THE ART OF THE HAUNT

Why soar below ground
in one inch of air like
under a hat? The moment you realize
you are not present
you are present. In my father's old bed
I dream I find an action
figure at the center of a labyrinth,
text my ex-wife from
the middle of the maze. The word *emotion*
comes from the Latin, *emovere*,
meaning "to disturb."
Like you die and all your clothes go
to Goodwill all at once.
Do they put the voice in storage
the way a person's burned hand
is sewn into his stomach
for safekeeping? When I was five
my mother put a man
on the moon, my father put a dog
on the sun. I snapped Polaroids of the hot
planets and the cold
heavens sketched in sidewalk chalk.
They say, *Luck today will be*
ability tomorrow. To transmit without
a satellite all of what
we could not say into art. What if
Christo stuffed the Holland Tunnel
with soft pretzels? What if

Christo stuffed the Chinatown
bus with survivalist kits
and we had to fight each
other for them? I've never had to
use a compass, never had to
survive—oh wait, I have.

BLUE YODEL #5

Someday your lasso will become the mouth of hell
and never shut.

Get along, little reader, like a mare indoors.

Like my grandmother's spirit jumping through the hoop
in the painted sky now beginning to smudge.

Some vanishing points are indefinite.
Like a ghost erased by a gust of wind.

Your boots lay empty near the door.
Your shadow, scrubbed from the desert floor.

Because there is fire
in our hearts, in hell there are probably nothing
but bellows. Great big ones.

On earth are the items left over from sagas:

One is a flip-flop floating on a puddle.
Another is a piece of tornado hail.

Here is a rifle to write with.
We'll be watching for the westward trail of its smoke.

NOSTALGIA DISORDER

I used to be a docent. I was how
the story got told. I said, *You are a human, but
you can also be saddled like a horse.*
The horse and its soldier always do that little waltz.
I used to jog past a bronze plaque
with braille on it. It read, *So and So
and His White Mare Stayed Here.*
The man woke, wrote a last-minute dispatch
on the back of a banknote
to win the second battle of Hackensack.

My great-grandfather
was a guard for a czar. After
they found him, the pockets of his wool coat
filled with silverware, he began
his era of exile, living only on expired love.
Far from the palace, he burned
all his letters for heat. Nudged his horse home
I don't know how many times.
When the Russians coined "far-sickness"
as an opposite illness, the only remedy
was to bury the sick man alive.

SEPTEMBER

We stand very still on apples
in the grass. Some yellow jackets

bomb America—the practical
women and men this morning

at the orchard. I hear a wren or
finch going berserk, no parts of

speech. What all poems reenact:
electricity brings the monster to life—

a jagged scar across every joint.
In the parking lot the whole

orchard behind us reappears
in the side-view mirror of a van.

I hear the tethered goat full of milk
ringing her bell, a one-note melody.

Under forsythia, a black cat
whips its black tail like *goddamn.*

LATE STYLE

You did not make yourself, I say
to the snowman outlasting the snow. A pile

of white organ meat melting
by the fence. I was eight when I squeezed

my brightest fish until an egg
popped out. You could say every egg

is meant to echo the sun. Right now
I have no children of my own.

From the roof of my dead father's home
I see with my Pre-Raphaelite eye,

through the anatomical stillness of pine trees,
the blue water towers of the next

three towns along the shore. The outcropping
of gray rocks facedown in the surf.

I see something flit between
two perfect waves. In here, his window drapes

darken the entire room until my
movements cue a sleeping computer

from its sleep—my father's final
Google search: 'pain down middle of chest.'

THREE

WHAT I SCREAMED INTO

Suitcase, radiator, nightfall, suitcase,
cantilever, underwear, zinnia, nightcap,
radiator, stethoscope, mascara,
heating duct, peonies, empty helmet,
I don't know, stethoscope, peonies, uniform,
wheelbarrow, radiator, empty boot,
all right, Lincoln tunnel, Holland tunnel,
gas tank, I confess, wet telephone,
tap water, hatbox, refrigerator, hatbox,
mink stole, Camel Lights, aftershave,
nonsense, crop circle, peach pit,
my fault, restaurant, your fries, my fries,
last of the hoarfrost, I'm sorry, Carolina,
intersection, bald eagle, I'm sorry,
cocktails, hornet's nest, nonsense,
leather chair, sunrise, thank you, not
yet, hairline, owl house, deer along the road,
door hinge, inch of hail, architecture,
front porch, I confess, tress pass,
my mistake, the landscape, thumbtacks on a map.

YOUR TIME HAS COME

The mouth is a fright because it's also the entertainer.

That's how drama works.

Your voice is an organ for once.

Intention, a story within a story. A freezer truck hauling

donor hearts across Connecticut.

Today I stay indoors, recite a poem in which raindrops

are pitting the snow

with impossibly quiet applause. I screen

the rerelease of *12 Angry Men*.

The American courthouse

was modeled after ancient baths: grayscale, sunlit pillars,

the iridescent breasts of pigeons—

a predictable brand. The fact is

personality is a luxury.

You just need to choose your confession style.

MERCURIAL

Say feelings
are provisional. Sun

on the other side

of the house now. I can hear
the neighbor
        boy trying
                to start his
        cello with a bow,

proof only
of our proximity.

                I am avoiding
a vice, tap
        the desk
        with a spoon. Music

would make sense. A new anthem

from a baby
grand
            rising like smoke
        from an ashtray fire.

I want to remember

that number.
                    Not all music
is movement.

          Some songs we break
into and then leave behind.

IF YOU MUST HIDE YOURSELF FROM LOVE

It is important to face the rear of the train
as it leaves the republic. Not that all

departing is yearning. First love is
a factory. We sleep in a bed that had once

been a tree. Nothing is forgotten.
Yet facts, over time, lose their charm,

warned a dying Plato. You have to isolate
the lies you love. Are we any less

photorealistic? I spot in someone's Face-
book sonogram a tiny dictum

full of syllogisms. One says: all kisses come
down to a hole in the skull,

toothpaste and gin; therefore your eyes
are bull—your mouth is a goal.

WILD LEMONS

We wake like bees and peel a lemon.
Then there is a glowing.
Do you want to eat it wedge by wedge?
Pull the pith off, keep the seeds.
Lift a blue crayon, ring
each other's mouths in blue.
We all live under a rule—
a lemon law for what's beyond repair:
our very first lovers doubled over
in grief like singers slumped
over tiny guitars. Now I remember
keeping wallet pictures,
feeling at times a curious despair.

Like somebody's father
I lay in the room where nobody is
and read in *Reader's Digest*
how lemon rind can help keep herbs
moist through winter, how
their cellular walls need to breathe.
Rind can also give a person
hives, horrible flying and dying
dreams in which a dead soul
won't leave the body until
a hunger develops. The bottom

of the feet. The face. Hands.
Where on your body would
you hide the last lemon
on earth? Lie down. Show me
on your dimply limbs.

RECEIPTS FOR ALL THOSE CLOUDS

I pour out the urn until the trees grow huge.
It's not morbid anymore
to work the proud ash. The body beyond itself.
A wren queries from the top of a pole.

Back away, the wind says, as if to explain
the idea of *good-bye* to a child
watching her loose balloon ascend
into the spokes of trees. What does it mean

to wait for the day to remake you,
or for a jet plane to fertilize a cloud?
We are forever being shot through
the dream hole. How we open and close

more slowly with age. *This is the life span.*
It is more fatherless the farther north you go.
Father, I have fallen in love
again. Like looking at a cloud and trying

to rise to meet it. It's this way
a cloud has, full of water and placebo.
I've seen people take the world
apart so that all distance is removed.

Loving, for them, was mostly
a mechanical thing, a way to stop time—
now we have to be unlocked
like a wristwatch pried open with a thorn.

FORESHORTENING

The boys practice dying of
                wounds in the lot
behind the bakery they will fasten
                        to one knee tourniquets
                made of limp baguettes, then ride
lime green skateboards
                not exactly toward home
                        each one an arrow shot
                up with a cricket on its tip
to be stabbed earthward. Boys
                for whom monsters
                        are the main idea
the tender ones whose teeth
                        you can't always see
                but are reminded of
once the terror is felt.

ESTATE SALE

Asleep beneath lacquer, a family of nails
buried in wood.

I auction off, from another century, a black-handled thing.

An out-of-focus photograph
of my under-a-pink-sunset father

arriving in the driveway with a tire iron
to take me back.

Today on the wet roof I spotted
half a songbird
the cat left for no one.

I rearranged my albums, opened a bucolic book
for its mention of birches.

Reader, I once visited Robert Frost's grave, saw the deep-set dirt
there.

Left for him
the meat of one walnut.

Asked only why the sickly snow, the little horse

who thinks it's queer
that darkness demands human attention.

Today the light is nobody's.

I auction off other things:
Hubcap. Deathbed. Defenestrated
business suits. A bulletproof book
about the Four Noble Truths.

Night coming on, I walk out beneath the great copper beech,

see some kids
doing kung fu in the cul-de-sac.

They startle
a muskrat and its five babies
back down into the sewer.

SORROW, ARCHITECTURE

Oh yes, a temporary house.
Garage doors open all night.
In each dark space we'll park
our new work. Imagine a portico
so high an elephant could fit
in the door. I've been reading

The Sorrow of Architecture, a book
about our lack of blueprints.
The difficulty of sorrow is how
it doesn't cohere, the unbroken
lines rubbing away over time.
Last month my father's heart

attack ended our very long talk
about sports, a career in divorce,
of making one's way to the coast
where all the best buildings
edge into nature. How a house,
property, is a horror.

When the tall junipers give
so much shade they make black.
When behind one house
is another the sun never finds.

A SUITABLE PERIOD OF TIME

They pack the heart in ice.
It won't last the night.
Like my three-years' dead cat
for a second coming back
to life in the side yard
whenever the robins collect.

Keep waiting, she is saying.
But when my life came back
to me it was like someone
coming to on linoleum tile,
the sound of a saw
in the neighborhood.

Tonight, I am meeting friends
for pizza, Cherry Cokes.
I coast on my bike, standing
up like a sail despite a head
cold. My helmet edits
out half the horizon.

The organs in my belly
blaze all night. The galaxy
pivots its starlight.
A public clock ticks. The day
moon burns through
the night moon and pulls
the sky close.

THE BYRONIC METHOD

It's going to be an interesting life.

The paper lamps are what I love.

I hope the woman reading the book

in my lap doesn't ever close it.

Even if the tips of her fingers turn black

I want to remember how her arms

make room for wings, rather than flanks.

I'm in my socks. She turns

each page, slightly tearing the tops.

It's a story about feeling like you're falling

backward off a moving train, and how

later everyone has a drink

and laughs about it. She has done this

before—read a player a book.

I close my eyes and picture an elevator

idling in my street. Outside, the leaves

of poplars, large pulmonary leaves

lie on the ground. The end.

NOTES

"The Art of the Haunt" is dedicated to Paul Mazza.

"In Vitro" ("Around the wreck of . . .") was inspired by and is dedicated to my late mentor, Jason Shinder.

"Receipts for All Those Clouds" is written for and because of Kelsea Habecker.

"Sorrow, Architecture" was inspired by and is dedicated to my late teacher and mentor, Liam Rector. He wrote a book of poetry carrying the title *The Sorrow of Architecture.*

"Sun & Urn" is for Matt Salerno.

"What I Screamed Into" borrows its essence from a poem by Elizabeth Hughey.

This book is dedicated to the memory of my late father, Peter Salerno.

Expired love